This Book
Belongs to

_____

_____

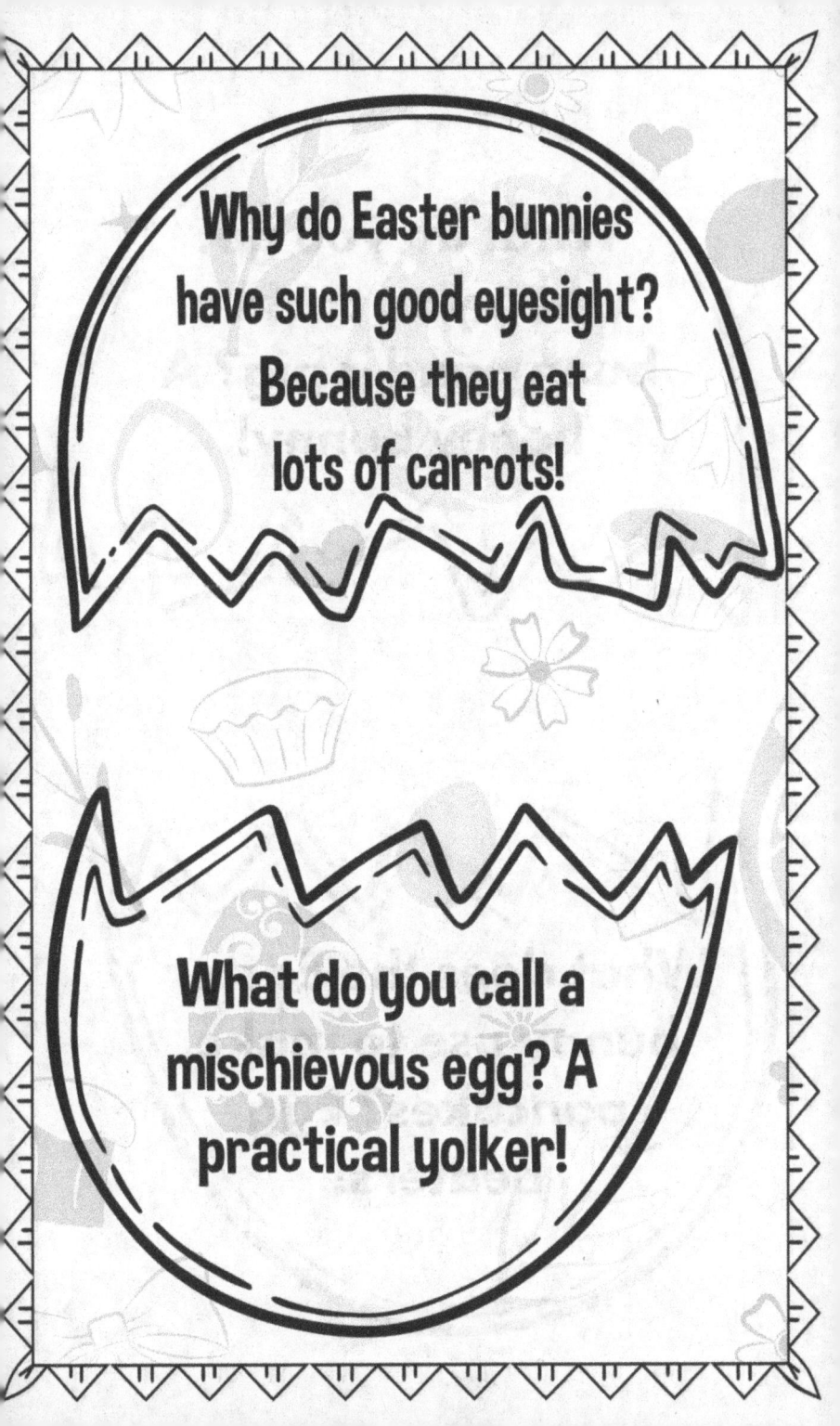

Why do Easter bunnies have such good eyesight? Because they eat lots of carrots!

What do you call a mischievous egg? A practical yolker!

What do you get when you cross a bunny and a pig? A honey bunny!

What does the Easter bunny use to make pancakes? Egg beaters!

What do you call an egg from outer space? An egg-straterrestrial!

What do you call a bunny that's really cool? A hip hopper!

Why did the Easter bunny cross the road? To get to the hop-side!

How does the Easter bunny stay fit? By doing egg-cercise!

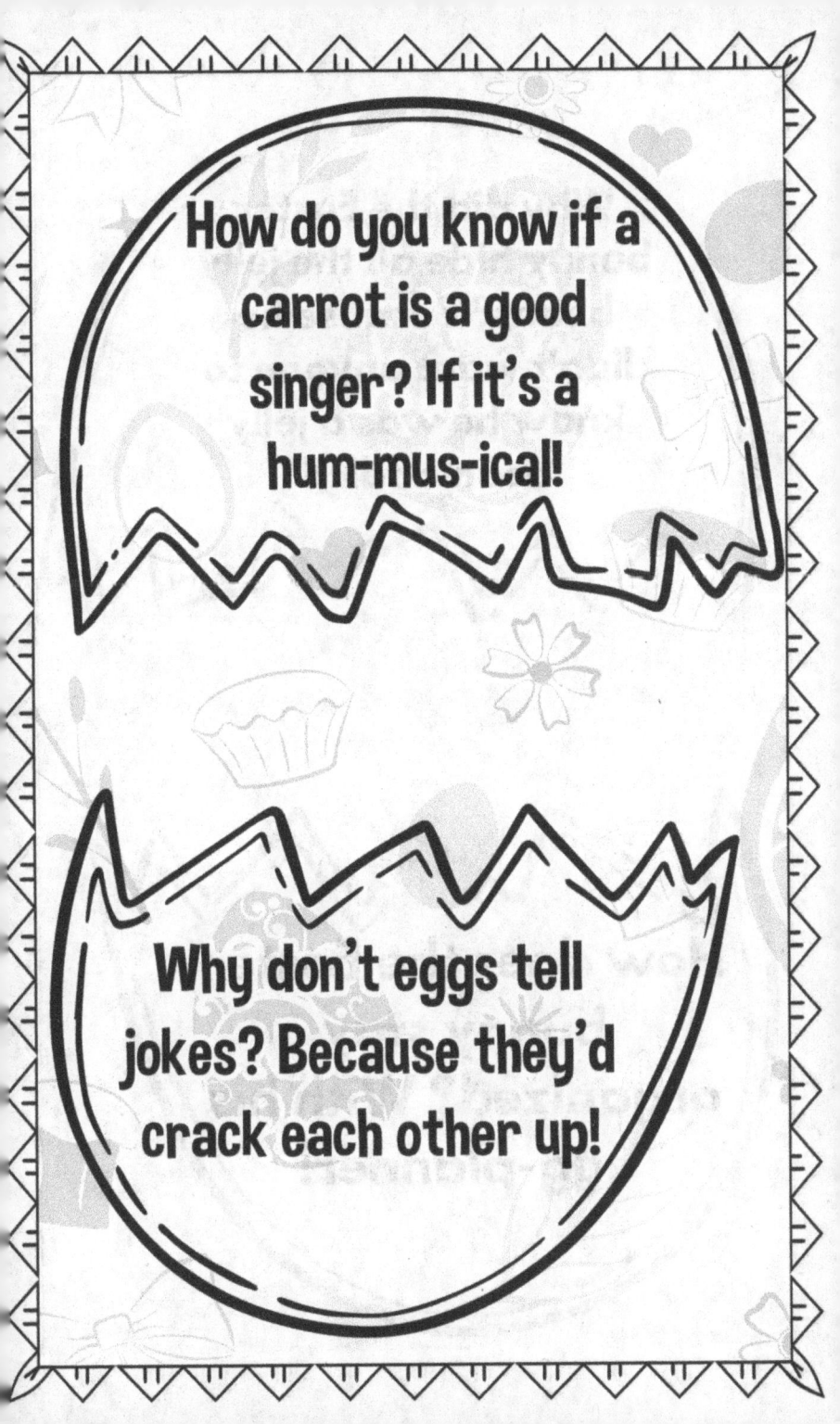

Why did the Easter bunny hide all the jelly beans? Because he didn't want anyone to know he was a jelly bean addict!

How does the Easter bunny stay organized? With his egg-planner!

How do you make a bunny float? Add ice cream and a hop of soda!

What do you call a bunny who tells jokes? A funny bunny!

How do you know if the Easter bunny has been using your computer? There are chocolate bunny footprints all over the keyboard!

What's the Easter bunny's favorite type of movie? Hop-eratic films!

How do you know if the Easter bunny has been using your computer? There are chocolate bunny footprints all over the keyboard!

What's the Easter bunny's favorite type of movie? Hop-eratic films!

How does the Easter bunny keep his fur looking good? With hare spray!

Why was the Easter bunny so upset? He was having a bad

What do you get when you cross an Easter egg with a caterpillar? A choco-laterpillar!

What do you call an Easter egg with a hole in it? A shell-abration!

Why did the Easter bunny refuse to eat breakfast? He was already eggs-hausted!

How do you know if an egg is good at tennis? If it can serve and volley!

Why did the Easter bunny refuse to share his chocolate eggs? He was feeling a bit shellfish!

What do you call a bunny that plays basketball? A slam dunkin' hare!

What do you get when you cross an Easter egg with a ghost? A chick who goes "boo-k, booo-k!"

What do you call a sleepy egg? Eggs-austed!

What do you get when you cross a bunny with a parrot? A bird that can hop and squawk!

Why did the Easter bunny refuse to take a bath? He didn't want to wash his hare!

What do you get when you cross an Easter bunny with a chef? A hop-culinary expert!

What do you call an Easter egg from a famous artist? An egg-spressionist!

How do you catch the Easter bunny? Hide in the bushes and make a noise like a carrot!

What do you call a rabbit who tells jokes? A funny bunny!

Why did the Easter bunny hide his eggs on the playground? To make them egg-stra playful!

What do you call an Easter egg from a famous singer? A yolk-tista!

Why did the Easter bunny cross the playground? To get to the other slide!

How does the Easter bunny stay fit? By doing egg-cercise!

What do you get when you cross an Easter bunny with a sailor? A hop-seaman!

Why did the Easter bunny go to the beach? To hop on some waves!

Why did the Easter egg hide from the other eggs? It was a little egg-centric!

What do you call a rabbit with fleas? Bugs Bunny!

Why did the Easter bunny join the circus? He was a natural acro-bunny!

What do you call an Easter egg from a famous athlete? A champ-egg-on!

What do you get when you cross an Easter egg with a dog? A golden retriever!

Why did the Easter bunny join the band? He loved the carrot-oke!

What do you call a rabbit that tells jokes on April Fool's Day? A funny bunny!

Why did the Easter egg hide in the grass? It was egg-scared!

Why did the Easter bunny bring a clock to the Easter egg hunt? To keep his hare on time!

What do you call a bunny with a cold? A hoppy nose!

How does the Easter bunny keep his fur looking good? With hare spray!

How does the Easter bunny keep his eggs safe? With egg-cryption!

What do you get when you cross an Easter bunny with a famous detective? Sherlock Hops!

What do you call a bunny that can hop really high? A bouncer!

What did the Easter bunny say when he was asked to do a magic trick? "Ta-da! Egg-sactly what you were expecting!"

What did the Easter bunny say to the carrot? "Nice gnawing you!"

Why did the Easter egg break up with the Easter bunny? Because it found someone better: the choco-late!

How do bunnies stay healthy? They egg-cercise and eat carrot-fully!

What do you get when you cross a bunny with a frog? A rabbit that ribbits!

Why did the Easter bunny have to wear glasses? He lost his contacts!

What do you get when you cross a bunny with a rooster? An egg-stra special delivery!

What's the Easter bunny's favorite type of music? Hip-hop!

What does the Easter bunny say when he's about to run out of candy? "Hop to it!"

What do you call an egg from outer space? An egg-straterrestrial!

What do you call an Easter bunny that loves to read? A book-hopper!

What do you call an Easter egg that tells jokes? A yolker!

Why did the Easter bunny bring a calculator to the Easter egg hunt? To count his eggs-act finds!

What do you get when you cross an Easter bunny with a pilot? A hare-plane!

Why did the Easter bunny put on a magic show? To show off his hare-raising tricks!

Why did the Easter bunny go to the spa? To relax and hop away his stress!

Why did the Easter bunny bring a magnifying glass to the Easter egg hunt? To make sure he didn't miss any egg-cellent hiding spots!

What do you call an Easter bunny who loves to skateboard? A hop-skater!

Why did the Easter bunny hide his eggs on the roof of the tallest building in town? To make them egg-streme!

Why did the Easter bunny hide his eggs in the cave? To make them egg-sotic!

Why did the Easter bunny bring a calculator to the Easter egg hunt? To count his egg-sact finds!

What do you call an Easter bunny who loves to make movies? A hop-tographer!

Why did the Easter bunny bring a compass to the Easter egg hunt? To find his way to the egg-citing prizes!

What do you get when you cross an Easter bunny with a teacher? A hop-educator!

Why did the Easter bunny cross the road twice? To prove he wasn't chicken!

What do you call a rabbit with fleas? Bugs Bunny!

What do you call a group of rabbits hopping backwards? A receding hare-line!

Why did the Easter egg refuse to come out of its shell? It was too chicken!

Why did the Easter bunny hide in the garden? He was egg-cited to see all the new plants!

What does the Easter bunny say when he wants to leave? "Hoppy trails to you!"

Why did the Easter bunny go to the psychiatrist? He had a lot of hare problems!

How does the Easter bunny decorate his house? With egg-shibits!

What do you get when you cross an Easter egg with a cow? A chocolate moo-sse!

How does the Easter bunny send messages? By hare-mail!

What do you get when you cross an Easter egg with a flower? An egg-stra special bouquet!

Why did the Easter bunny go to the doctor? He had a bad hare day!

Why did the Easter bunny paint his eggs with bright colors? He wanted them to egg-spress themselves!

What do you call a bunny with a lot of money? A million-hare!

Why did the Easter bunny paint his eggs with spots? He wanted to make them egg-ceptional!

Why did the Easter bunny get a ticket? He was caught hare-speeding!

What do you get when you cross an Easter egg with a duck? An egg-stra cute quack!

What do you get when you cross a bunny with a deer? A hare-antelope!

Why did the Easter bunny join the basketball team? He was a great hop-shooter!

Why did the Easter bunny go to space? He wanted to visit the Milky Way!

Why did the Easter bunny refuse to eat breakfast? He was already eggs-hausted!

What do you call an Easter egg from a famous artist? A hatch-a-lyst!

Why did the Easter bunny hide his eggs in a pyramid? He wanted to be egg-sotic!

Why did the Easter bunny cross the bridge? To get to the other side!

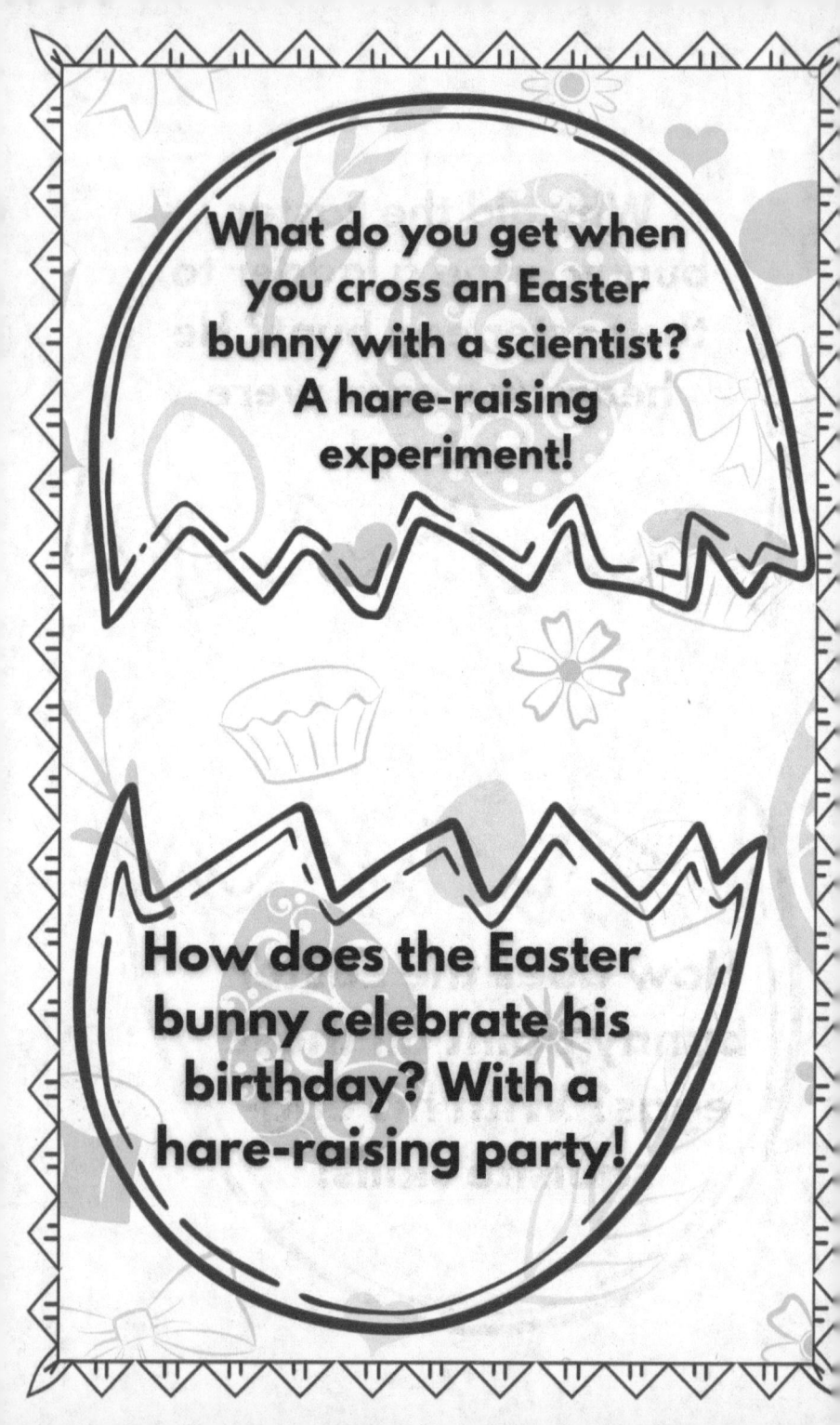

What do you get when you cross an Easter bunny with a scientist? A hare-raising experiment!

How does the Easter bunny celebrate his birthday? With a hare-raising party!

What do you get when you cross an Easter bunny with a rock star? A hare-raising concert!

What do you call a bunny that tells really bad jokes? A punny hare!

Why did the Easter bunny join the circus? He loved the acro-bunny-tics!

What do you get when you cross an Easter egg with a bird? A tweet-egg!

What do you call an Easter egg from the 1980s? An egg-citing blast from the past!

Why did the Easter bunny go to the dentist? He had a cavity bunny!

Why did the Easter bunny bring a basket to the Easter egg hunt? He needed something to carry his egg-citing finds!

Why did the Easter bunny go to school? To learn how to egg-spand his horizons!

What do you call an Easter bunny who can jump higher than a house? Hop-solutely amazing!

Why did the Easter bunny bring a carrot to the dance? To put a little hop in his step!

What do you get when you cross an Easter bunny with a magician? A hare-raising trick!

What do you call an Easter egg from a famous actor? A hollywood egg!

What do you get when you cross an Easter bunny with a caterer? A hare-raising feast!

Why did the Easter bunny cross the road twice? To prove he wasn't a chicken!

What do you get when you cross an Easter bunny with a football player? A hare-dy quarterback!

Why did the Easter bunny go to the gym? He wanted to work on his bunny hops!

Why did the Easter bunny bring a map to the Easter egg hunt? He didn't want to get lost in the woods!

Why did the Easter bunny join the football team? He was the hareline!

Why did the Easter bunny hide in the tree? Because he was a little egg-scared!

What do you get when you cross an Easter bunny with a singer? A hop-star!

Why did the Easter bunny hide his eggs in the orchard? He wanted to make them apple-egg-tizers!

What do you get when you cross an Easter bunny with a painter? A hop-painter!

Why did the Easter bunny bring a ladder to the Easter egg hunt? To climb to the top of the egg hunt leaderboard!

What do you call a bunny that tells jokes on Easter? The funny bunny!

Why did the Easter bunny hide in the chicken coop? To take a break from all the Easter egg hiding!

What do you call an Easter bunny that loves to read? A book-hopper!

Why did the Easter bunny bring a flashlight to the Easter egg hunt? To find the hidden eggs in the dark!

What do you call an Easter egg that likes to play soccer? A kickster!

What do you get when you cross an Easter bunny with a police officer? A hop-stable law-enforcer!

What do you call an Easter bunny who loves to tell jokes? A hare-y comedian!

What do you get when you cross an Easter bunny with a personal trainer? A hare-raising workout!

Why did the Easter bunny hide his eggs in the freezer? To keep them egg-cold!

Why did the Easter bunny bring a trampoline to the Easter egg hunt? To hop over the competition!

What do you get when you cross an Easter bunny with a detective? A hop-sleuth!

Why did the Easter bunny hide his eggs in the gym? To make them egg-specially fit!

What do you get when you cross an Easter bunny with a farmer? A hop-gardener!

Why did the Easter bunny hide his eggs on the roof? To egg-scape the Easter egg hunters!

What do you get when you cross an Easter bunny with a musician? A hop-tune!

Why did the Easter bunny hide his eggs in the mountain? He wanted them to be egg-treme!

What do you call an Easter bunny who loves to dance hip-hop? A hopper!

Why did the Easter bunny bring a bell to the Easter egg hunt? To hop in the rhythm!

Why did the Easter bunny go to the tailor? He wanted a custom-made bunny suit!

What do you get when you cross an Easter bunny with a computer programmer? A hare-raising app!

How does the Easter bunny paint all those eggs? With his hare brush!

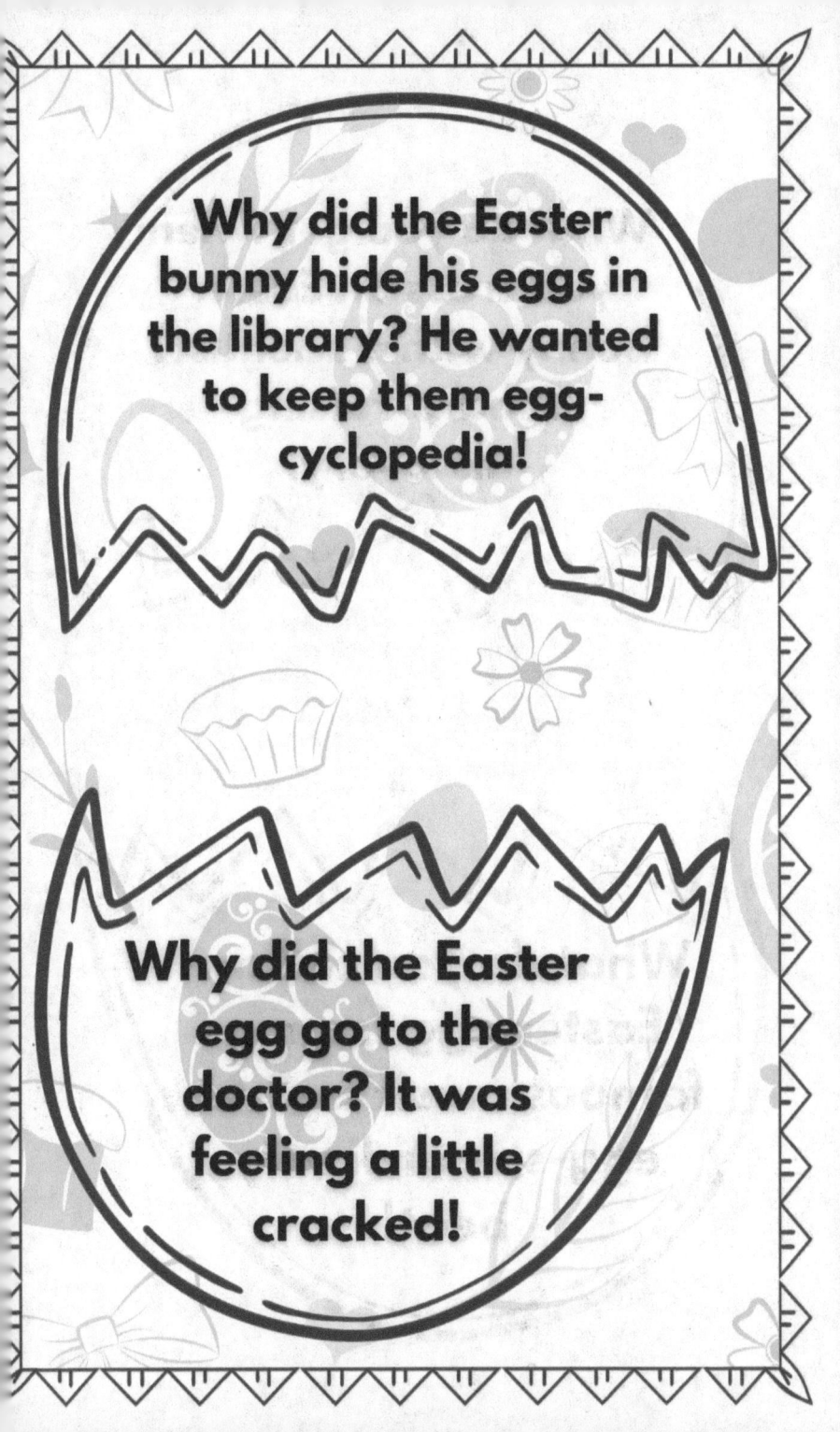

Why did the Easter bunny hide his eggs in the library? He wanted to keep them egg-cyclopedia!

Why did the Easter egg go to the doctor? It was feeling a little cracked!

Why did the Easter bunny hide his eggs in the garden? He wanted to make sure they were organ-egg!

What do you get when you cross an Easter bunny with a chef? A hare-raising meal!

What do you get when you cross an Easter bunny with a gardener? A hare-raising harvest!

Why did the Easter bunny wear sunglasses? Because he didn't want to get egg-glare!

What do you get when you cross an Easter bunny with a racecar driver? A hare-raising finish!

Why did the Easter bunny cross the road on a skateboard? To get to the half-pipe!

Why did the Easter bunny bring a hammer to the Easter egg hunt? To crack open the eggs!

What do you call an Easter bunny who tells jokes on TV? A hare-lerious comedian!

Why did the Easter bunny bring a watch to the Easter egg hunt? He wanted to hop on time!

What do you get when you cross an Easter bunny with a monster? A hop-tical illusion!

What do you get when you cross an Easter bunny with a fireman? A hare-raising rescue!

What do you call an Easter bunny who's really good at puzzles? A hare-brained genius!

Why did the Easter bunny bring a camera to the Easter egg hunt? To capture all his egg-citing moments!

What do you get when you cross an Easter bunny with a magician? A hare-raising illusion!

Why did the Easter bunny bring a broom to the Easter egg hunt? To sweep up all the egg shells!

Why did the Easter bunny hide his eggs in the library? He wanted to keep them egg-silent!

Why did the Easter bunny hide his eggs in the clouds? He wanted them to be egg-celestial!

What do you get when you cross an Easter bunny with a doctor? A hare-raising diagnosis!